# Teddy B, Teddy B, Tell Me What You Wanna Be

Written by Katherine Gallo   Illustrated by Jennette Mills

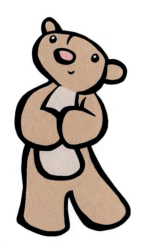

© 2020 Jennette Mills.  All rights reserved.
For ordering information or permissions requests, please contact:

https://www.twotreesart.com

Printed in the United States of America
ISBN 978-1-7328991-4-8

## *Dedication*

To my heart, my inspiration & my rainbow baby,
I dedicate these pages of imagination & play to you.
You can truly be anything you want to be, my Teddy B. ♥

*— Katherine Gallo (aka Mama)*

# Teddy B, Teddy B,
## tell me whatcha' wanna be

# Teddy B, Teddy B,
## Tell me what you wanna be

# Teddy B, Teddy B,
## tell me what you wanna be

# Teddy B, Teddy B,
## Tell me what you wanna be

# Teddy B, Teddy B,
## tell me what you wanna be

# Teddy B, Teddy B,
## tell me what you wanna be

# Teddy B, Teddy B,
## Tell me what you wanna be

# Teddy B, Teddy B,
## tell me what you wanna be

# Teddy B, Teddy B,
## Tell me what you wanna be

# Teddy B, Teddy B,
## tell me what you wanna be

# TEDDY B, TEDDY B,
## TELL ME WHAT YOU WANNA BE

# Teddy B, Teddy B,
## Tell me what you wanna be

# Do you wanna be a

*Sssssss*

# Snake?

# Teddy B, Teddy B,
## Tell me what you wanna be

# Teddy B, Teddy B,
## Tell me what you wanna be

# Teddy B, Teddy B,
## Tell me what you wanna be

# Teddy B, Teddy B,
## Tell me what you wanna be

# Teddy B, Teddy B,
## Tell me what you wanna be

# Teddy B, Teddy B,
## tell me what you wanna be

What's Next for Teddy B?

Find out
& Get a FREE
Teddy B
Coloring Printout
with the QR code below!

Scan the code
Find more fun @:
twotreesart.com

Made in the USA
Middletown, DE
17 December 2020